Paulo's Parachute Mission

An Aerospace Engineering Story

Written by the Engineering is Elementary Team

Illustrated by Keith Favazza

Chapter One | No Place Like Home

Paulo peered into the last cardboard box in his bedroom. Hiding in the shadowed corner was his soccer ball. He bent down to take it out, but stopped, his hand hovering a few inches above it. Once that ball was out of the box, he would be completely unpacked. The move would be final.

"Hey, Paulo, I'm going to hang out with the neighbors," Paulo's older sister, Júlia, called from down the hallway. "Have you seen my bag?"

Relieved for the distraction, Paulo headed toward the rustling he heard in the kitchen. "Nope, haven't seen it," Paulo said as he rounded the corner. "Júlia?" he called. The kitchen was empty. "Júlia?"

"Found it!" Júlia sprang up from behind a mountain of

boxes and held up her bag as proof. "Hey, you should come meet everyone. It'll be fun."

"No, thanks. I think I'll stay here," Paulo said.

"Suit yourself," Júlia said. She walked over to Paulo and squeezed his shoulders. "It's gonna be okay, you know?"

Paulo looked at the floor and nodded. "I know."

It had been two months since the day Paulo's parents announced the family was moving. He had been eating lunch with Mãe, Pai, Júlia, and his best friend, Andre. The smell of *feijoada*—salty pork, beans, and spices—filled the room. Paulo and Andre had been talking about the big soccer game coming up. That was when Pai broke the news that they were moving.

"*Alcantara*?" Júlia had asked. "Do people even *live* there?"

"Of course people live there," Pai had said. "It will be a great adventure. You two have almost never been out of this city. You'll get to see a whole new world—plants and animals. And the sky! You'll be amazed at how brilliant the stars look without the lights of the city masking their glow."

Paulo had barely heard Pai. How could they leave Brasilia? The big, bustling capital city was the only place Paulo had ever lived. His school, his friends—everything was in Brasilia.

"But . . . why?" Paulo finally managed to say.

Mãe had placed her hand over Paulo's. "Your Pai and I have been offered a chance to work with the scientists and other engineers at the space launch pad in Alcantara. We'll be on a team designing a craft that will travel into space. It will help scientists make new discoveries. Isn't that exciting?" she had asked, squeezing his fingers.

Chapter Two | A New Friend?

Paulo hadn't felt excited that afternoon. Now that he was sitting in their new kitchen, he still didn't feel excited. He didn't want to be in this new house, and he didn't want to make any new friends. Why would he need to? He already had Andre, his soccer team, and his friends at school in Brasilia.

There was one more reason that Paulo hadn't wanted this change. He hadn't mentioned it to Mãe or Pai. He didn't even like to think about it himself. Paulo was afraid that people in this new town might think he was . . . different. He had been born with one hand that had three fingers instead of five. It hardly affected anything Paulo did, but it didn't look the same as everyone else's hands. In Brasilia, people knew Paulo and were comfortable with his hand. They knew that his hand didn't matter—that he was just Paulo. But he couldn't help thinking that the people in his new town wouldn't know that.

Paulo nudged open the screen door and stepped outside. He still found the quiet yard surrounding their new house strange—so different from the tall buildings and streets that ringed their old apartment building. For the past few nights Paulo had sat outside and gazed up at the sky. *At least I still have the stars*, he thought. In Brasilia Paulo had loved looking at the stars each night before he fell asleep. Some people used holidays or changes in weather to mark

the passing seasons. Paulo used the movement of the stars. He knew that when the Southern Cross was framed by his window, school would be starting soon. And when he could see the red of Betelgeuse and the blue of Rigel with Orion's belt in the middle, he knew spring was just around the corner. When Paulo looked out the window on any given night, everything he could see, from the stars to the moon to the planets, seemed totally still. But as the seasons passed, Paulo could watch the movement of lots of stars and planets in space just by looking through that window. Now, out here in Alcantara, the stars seemed like familiar friends.

Paulo stood and walked around the yard. He spotted a

box next to the corner of the house and peered inside. Gardening tools, a wrench set, and . . . *how'd that get in here?* The object he pulled out looked like an old scrap of fabric. But it was much more than that to Paulo. He and Andre had made the *paraquedas*—parachute—to help them send messages to each other at night. They'd lived in the same apartment building, and Paulo's room had been just above Andre's. When they were supposed to be asleep, they used the *paraquedas* to send secret messages to each other. Andre would slide his messages into a little container and toss them up for Paulo to catch from his window. Paulo would attach his replies to the *paraquedas* and drop them down. Paulo's heart fell as he remembered the old apartment and his friend.

He held the *paraquedas* up and then let it go, watching it drift slowly down to the ground. *No use for this now*, Paulo thought. He picked up the *paraquedas* again, then noticed someone at the edge of the yard.

Paulo stared at the boy. The boy stared back. Neither one spoke. Finally, Paulo broke the silence. "*Oi.*"

"*Oi*. Um . . . your sister, Júlia? She was talking to my sister and she said that you're twelve? I am, too."

Paulo nodded and raised an eyebrow. The boy continued. "She says you like soccer? And I've been looking for someone to practice with . . . " The boy trailed off.

Paulo tried not to roll his eyes. He'd told Júlia he didn't want to meet the other kids in the neighborhood. The boy was looking back at Paulo with wide, hopeful eyes. Not sure what else to do, Paulo stuck out his left hand—his five-

fingered hand—to introduce himself. Paulo almost always used his left hand to shake hands with new people, even though he knew most people would be expecting his right. "I'm Paulo."

The boy put out his right hand, then—looking confused—switched to offer his left. He smiled and said, "I'm Lucas. Did you make that *paraquedas*?"

"Uh, yeah," Paulo said. "I made it with a friend of mine."

"It's neat," Lucas said. "What else do you like to do? Do you want to come kick the ball around? I have a goal set up in my backyard."

"No," Paulo said. The smile disappeared from Lucas's face. Feeling guilty, Paulo quickly added, "I still have a lot of unpacking to do. Maybe we could do it tomorrow."

"Okay, yeah," Lucas said. "I'll come by tomorrow. Good luck with the unpacking," he said, then turned and jogged off. Paulo stepped back inside and let the door swing shut. *Júlia is in big trouble*, he thought.

Chapter Three | Second Impressions

The next day Paulo spent all morning trying to come up with an excuse so he wouldn't have to play soccer with Lucas. More unpacking to do? Didn't feel well? Tired? *Those excuses will work for a little while*, Paulo thought, *but they're not going to solve the problem*.

Finally Paulo settled on a plan. He would go, kick the soccer ball and talk to Lucas for a bit, and then explain that he didn't need any more friends. He had plenty, back in Brasilia.

Right after lunch Lucas knocked on the kitchen door. As they walked down the dusty road to Lucas's backyard, Paulo realized he was hiding his three-fingered hand against his side. He felt his face getting hot. *I shouldn't be embarrassed*, he reminded himself. Paulo made a conscious effort to swing his hand normally as he walked. Paulo glanced sideways at Lucas, but Lucas didn't seem to notice either Paulo's worrying or his hand.

"This is it," Lucas said. He pointed to a goal: two large tree branches stuck into the ground. A soccer ball sat between the posts. Lucas dribbled the ball and gently kicked it to Paulo.

"Why did your family move here?" Lucas asked as they kicked the ball back and forth.

"For my parents' jobs. They're aerospace engineers," Paulo explained.

"Wow! They go into space?" Lucas asked.

"No, they're not astronauts," Paulo said.

"Aw," Lucas said, his excitement fading. "It would be awesome if they were."

"They get to work with astronauts sometimes," Paulo said quickly. He was annoyed at his urge to impress Lucas. Why did he care what Lucas thought if he didn't want him as a friend anyway? "They work on teams that design spacecraft or parts of other things that fly, like planes. Right now they're working on a *paraquedas* that will be part of a spacecraft," Paulo continued.

"Like the one you had in your backyard?" Lucas asked, popping the ball from one knee to the other.

"Kind of," Paulo said. "When the rockets land, something has to slow them down so they don't hit the ground too hard. That's where the *paraquedas* comes in. In Brasilia my parents teach a whole course at the university about drag—air resistance—and how things fall through the air or the atmospheres on other planets. Well, they did when we lived there."

Just then Lucas gave the ball a quick kick and it flew off to the left. Paulo reached over his head and grabbed the ball with both hands.

"Oh," Lucas said. He was staring at Paulo's hand, a look of surprise on his face. Paulo dropped the ball and stood still for a moment, looking at the ground.

"I've never been to Brasilia," Lucas said. "What's it like?"

Paulo dribbled

the ball between his feet a few times before looking up at Lucas. *Was he not going to say anything about his hand?*

"The city's great," Paulo said. "There are always a lot of people in parks and restaurants."

"It must be pretty different from here," Lucas continued.

"Yeah," Paulo said. "My best friend, Andre, and I were always out with friends. There was so much to do." Silence hung between them for a few moments.

"There are things to do here, too," Lucas offered. "Have you walked around outside of town yet? We could do that this afternoon if you want."

"I don't know," Paulo said. *This is my chance,* he thought to himself. *I should just tell him that I don't need any more friends.* Paulo opened his mouth to explain, but a nagging feeling in his stomach stopped him. "Mãe told me not to be gone too long," Paulo mumbled. "I should really get back now."

"Oh, sure," Lucas said quickly, bouncing the soccer ball from his toe to his knee and back again. "It's okay—we can go this weekend. It'll be great!"

Chapter Four | A *Capuaçu* Mission

Paulo managed to avoid Lucas the next day in school. Now all he had to do was make it through the trip home. As Paulo walked up his street, he saw Pai sitting on the front step. Mãe was there, too. No . . . not Mãe. Paulo groaned. Lucas!

"*Oi*!" Pai called as Paulo walked into the yard. "There you are! You should've walked home with Lucas. You would've gotten here faster."

"Yeah," Lucas said. "I realized you didn't know the shortcut home and I wanted to stop by to make sure you made it! I'll walk home with you next week."

"Shortcut," Paulo muttered as he joined them on the stoop.

"I didn't see you at school today," Lucas said. "Even at lunch. On Monday I'll show you around if you want."

"Lucas was just telling me about some of the interesting trees nearby," Pai said. "I was thinking the two of you could take a trip to get us some *capuaçu*. If you bring some back I bet I could convince Mãe to make some of her famous ice cream. What do you say?"

"Sounds great!" Lucas said.

Paulo couldn't believe this. *No!* he was shouting in his head. *It's not great!* But somehow, "Yeah. Sounds good," is what actually came out of his mouth.

"I should head home," Lucas said, "but I'll come get you tomorrow, okay?"

Paulo watched Lucas walk to the edge of the yard

before turning to Pai. "First Júlia, now you," Paulo said. "Why does everybody want me to hang out with Lucas?"

"It'll do you good to start meeting some kids your own age," Pai said.

"I don't need to meet anyone," Paulo said. "I have plenty of friends already."

"Fine," Pai said. "I'll make you a deal. Go with Lucas to get the *capuaçu*. If you really don't want to be friends with him after that, I won't make you."

"You promise you won't say anything about it after that?" Paulo asked. Pai nodded. "Okay," Paulo said. "It's a deal."

Chapter Five | Crash Landing

"Wake up!" Pai called as he opened the door of Paulo's room. "Time to get moving."

Paulo barely cracked one eye open. "What time is it?" he asked, throwing his arm over his face.

"Time for exploring!" Pai said. "Come on. Lucas will be here soon."

"Okay, okay," Paulo mumbled. He threw off his sheet and swung his feet onto the floor. "I didn't realize exploring had to start so early," he muttered. He brushed past Pai and headed into the bathroom.

Half an hour later Paulo and Lucas were walking toward the trees on the edge of town. Looking back Paulo saw the tile roofs of all the houses blending together to form red stripes along the edges of the streets.

"Here we are," Lucas said. "A *capuaçu* tree!" Huge, waxy leaves as long as Paulo's arm sprouted from the gnarled branches, making a bushy tuft at the top of the tree. The round, cream-colored *capuaçu* were about the size of Paulo's soccer ball.

"Great," Paulo said. "I'll just climb up and grab one. Then we can head back." The bark was rough under Paulo's hands as he pulled himself up the trunk. "I think I've got it," Paulo said, stretching his arm toward a melon. As soon as he had a good grip on it, he began to twist and pull down on the fruit. With a snap Paulo broke the *capuaçu* off the tree and held it in one hand.

"Okay, I'm going to drop this down to you. Ready?"

"Ready," Lucas said.

Paulo gently tossed the fruit toward the spot where Lucas was standing.

"Whoa!" Lucas called as the fruit flew by, narrowly missing him and crashing onto the ground. With a crack the melon broke open, splattering on the ground. Even from up in the tree, Paulo could see dirt and twigs clinging to the fruit.

"Nice catch," Paulo called. "No wonder you stick to soccer!"

"Hey, it's not my fault! You're pelting me with fruit," Lucas said with a laugh.

"I didn't, though," said Paulo. "I guess when I dropped it, gravity just took over." Paulo scanned the branches around him and sighed as he began scooting down the tree. "I don't see any others that I can reach. We'll have to find another tree."

"You know what we need?" Lucas asked. "Your *paraquedas*!"

"That thing?" Paulo scoffed as he reached the ground.

"It won't work. The *capuaçu* is too heavy. Even with the *paraquedas* attached, the fruit would still crash."

"We could change the *paraquedas*, though," Lucas said. "If your parents can make a *paraquedas* that stops a spaceship from crashing, we've got to be able to make one for the fruit. What was that you were talking about the other day? Drag? How does that work?"

Paulo wrinkled his brow as he tried to remember some of the things he'd heard Mãe and Pai discuss. "I think

DRAG

GRAVITY

it has to do with atmosphere. Here on Earth we call our atmosphere air. Even though we can't see air, air is made up of stuff," Paulo said. "When something falls through our atmosphere, it pushes away the air in its path."

"Huh?" Lucas asked.

"I think it's like this," Paulo said. "If you wanted to walk quickly down a crowded street, there would be lots of people in your way. You'd bump up against people in the crowd, and they'd bump you back."

Lucas nodded. "The crowd slows you down."

"Exactly," Paulo said. "When something is falling through the atmosphere, it's kind of like that. The thing that is falling pushes against the air, and the air pushes back—that's called drag. We need to create more drag on the *capuaçu* so that it falls slowly enough to land on the ground without breaking."

"We'll have to make a *paraquedas* that's a lot bigger than the one you had in your yard. We can definitely make this work," Lucas said.

Paulo couldn't help smiling a little bit. Lucas never gave up! Paulo had to admit he kind of liked it. "Yeah," Paulo said. "I guess you're right. Let's go make a *paraquedas*."

Chapter Six | A *Paraquedas* Plan

As the boys jogged toward Paulo's house, Paulo remembered something he'd heard Mãe and Pai talk about a hundred times at the dinner table. "You know," Paulo said, "real engineers have to fix and change the technologies they design all the time."

"Yeah, but they work on important technologies, like spaceships and stuff," Lucas said. "We're just working on a little *paraquedas*."

"It's still a technology, though," Paulo said. "Pai always says that a technology is any thing or process that people design to help solve a problem. If we design our *paraquedas* well, it will help us solve the problem of getting the *capuaçu* out of the tree without smashing."

"That will be the hard part—figuring out how to design it so it works," Lucas said.

Paulo had a sudden flash. "We can use the engineering design process!"

"The what?" Lucas asked.

"It's the way my parents solve problems at work," Paulo said. "We can ask Mãe and Pai about it when we get home."

When the boys reached the yard, the *paraquedas* was still on the step where Paulo had left it.

Paulo held up the *paraquedas* for Lucas to see. "There are really only three parts," he said. "The top is the canopy, the suspension lines are in the middle, and the load, or the weight it's carrying, is attached at the bottom."

"So we need all three parts," Lucas said. "But we could change some things about them—like the canopy's material."

"Or its shape," Paulo said.

"It sounds just like

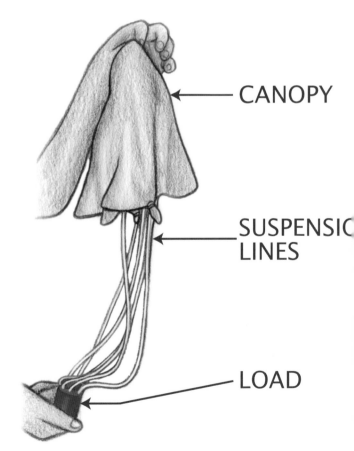

CANOPY

SUSPENSION LINES

LOAD

I'm at work!" Mãe said as she stepped outside. "What are you boys up to?"

Paulo explained their plan to redesign the *paraquedas* and gather *capuaçu*. "And I told Lucas about the engineering design process, but I couldn't remember all the steps."

"That will really be helpful as you're designing," Mãe said. "First you need to ask questions, like the questions about size, shape, and materials I heard you asking."

"I asked Paulo a bunch of questions about drag and atmosphere, too."

"Great," said Mãe. "It sounds like you're almost ready to start the next step: imagine. You imagine lots of different solutions, then choose one and make a detailed plan. Then you create your *paraquedas*, test it, and improve it."

"So you use all of those steps in your job?" Lucas asked.

"We do," said Mãe. "We have to do a lot of testing and improving, especially if what we're designing—a *paraquedas* or airplane or spacecraft—is going to travel through space or be used on another planet. Every material and part size and shape have to be designed carefully. Look over toward the launch pad," Mãe said, pointing high above the trees and houses. Paulo could see the huge tower with the green and black flag of Brazil painted on the top. Rising from the launch pad was the craft that Mãe and Pai were working on. "Why do you think the rocket is cone-shaped on the top?"

"Maybe because the rocket needs to travel really quickly through the air—through our atmosphere—to get into space," Lucas said.

"Exactly," Mãe said. "With a rocket, we want to create as little drag as possible. But with a *paraquedas*—"

"We want a lot of drag!" Lucas said. "The shape of a *paraquedas* is very different."

"Right again," Mãe said. "And when aerospace engineers think about drag, we don't just think about shape. We have to think about the atmosphere—the layer of gases—surrounding the planet that the craft will go to, and how that atmosphere might be different from the atmosphere here on Earth."

"How would you design a *paraquedas* that would work on Mars?" Lucas asked.

"You're really starting to sound like an engineer," Mãe said. "A lot of the time, aerospace engineers have to design technologies that will be used on other planets. But we can't visit other planets to test our designs. Sometimes we can model what it will be like on other planets, or use what we know about the two environments to design something that would work on a planet like Mars."

"Isn't the atmosphere on Mars a lot thinner than our

atmosphere?" Paulo asked.

"That's right," Mãe said. "The thickness of the atmosphere affects the amount of drag. The thinner atmosphere on Mars means there is less drag than here on Earth. So things fall more quickly on Mars than on Earth. You'd have to make a much bigger *paraquedas* to slow down the fall."

"But then how would you fit it in the spacecraft?" asked Lucas.

"Another great question," Mãe said. "You see, we don't only have to think about how the *paraquedas* will work. We also have to think about the strength of the materials that we're using and whether the final design will fit in the space that's available in the rocket. There are many different criteria to consider. Each design is unique to the place where it will be used and the criteria and goals we have."

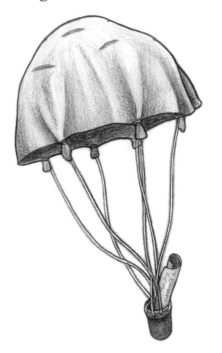

"We have a goal for our *paraquedas*, too," Lucas said. "To help us collect some *capuaçu*."

"Let's get started!" said Paulo.

Chapter Seven | *Paraquedas* Partners

Later that afternoon, after brainstorming many different *paraquedas* designs, Paulo and Lucas decided on one they thought would work well. They drew a plan and listed the materials they would need. Then they created their *paraquedas*.

"I have an idea! We can attach this bucket to the *paraquedas* to test it so we don't break another *capuaçu* if it doesn't work," Lucas said. "And maybe we need to add some rocks as a test load. Should we give it a try?"

"Yeah, let's see how it works," Paulo said.

Lucas stood on a chair on the stoop, held out his arm, and dropped the *paraquedas*. The bucket hit the ground with a thud, and the rocks tumbled out. Paulo looked at Lucas, his nose crinkled. "That *paraquedas* slowed the load down a little bit, but I think we have to do better if we want to make sure the fruit doesn't crack or bruise."

"Maybe this will make a better canopy," Lucas said, holding up a scrap of a different material. "It doesn't have as many little holes in it as the other material. I think this one will create more drag and fall more slowly."

"I think you're right," Paulo said. "Let's redesign it using that material."

Lucas untied the old canopy and put the new one in its place. "I just have to attach a few suspension lines to it and then we can test it," Lucas said. His brow wrinkled as

he concentrated on tying a knot. "Paulo, can you give me a hand with this?" he asked.

"Um, easier said than done," Paulo said, holding up his three-fingered hand.

Lucas looked up, a deep blush spreading from his collar to the top of his forehead. "I . . . um . . . "

"It's okay," Paulo said, punching him lightly on the shoulder. "I'm joking. Give me the string."

Lucas smiled. "Oh, man," he said. "I would've felt awful if you were serious."

"Don't worry," Paulo said. "There really aren't many things that are hard for me to do because of my hand. I'm used to it looking different. You'll get used to it, too."

The next day Paulo found himself again in the *capuaçu* tree, putting a fruit into the bucket tied to their improved *paraquedas*. Lucas stood on the ground, looking up into the green leaves of the tree.

"Okay," Paulo said. "Are you ready?"

"Ready!" Lucas said. "Let it go!"

Paulo released the *paraquedas*. He held his breath as he watched the *capuaçu* float down like a leaf in the wind. Finally, with a soft glide, the fruit landed gently on the ground.

"We did it!" Lucas called. Paulo climbed down and

then jumped the last few feet from the tree and ran over to inspect the fruit for himself.

"Good job!" Paulo said. Lucas and Paulo slapped hands to congratulate each other. It wasn't until they were walking home that Paulo realized he had used his three-fingered hand.

"We did it!" Paulo called across the yard to Mãe, Pai, and Júlia.

"Not one scratch or bruise on it!" Lucas said, holding up the *capuaçu*.

"A successful mission!" Pai said. "This calls for a celebration. Now, if we only knew someone who made really great *capuaçu* ice cream . . . "

"That's my cue," Mãe said. "I think I can have some ready by dinnertime. How does that sound?" she asked Paulo and Lucas.

"Great!" Paulo said.

"I know some other people who would like having ice cream with us," Júlia said, turning toward Paulo. "What do you say? Can I invite the other neighbors, too?"

"Yeah," Lucas said. "It'll be your 'welcome to the neighborhood' party."

"Sounds good to me," Paulo said.

"Hey, you know what we could do 'til then?" Lucas

asked. "Sometimes on the weekend there are soccer games in the field by school. Want to go see if anyone's playing?"

"Yeah!" Paulo said. "Let me grab my stuff." He ran down the hallway to his room, where the last box from the move still held his soccer ball. This time, a big smile spread across Paulo's face as he grabbed the ball and ran outside.

Design Your Own Parachute

Can you design a parachute to help an object travel safely from the top of a stairway to the ground? Your goal is to create a parachute that slows the falling speed of your object to five feet per second.

Materials

- ☐ Stopwatch or clock with second hand
- ☐ String
- ☐ Scissors
- ☐ Tape
- ☐ Aluminum foil
- ☐ Tissue paper
- ☐ Copy paper
- ☐ Small toy or other object
- ☐ Measuring tape
- ☐ Plastic bag

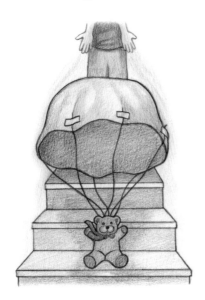

Ask and Imagine

Choose a safe spot ten feet off the ground to use as your testing location. A stair on a stairway might be a good place. Use a measuring tape to make sure the spot is the right height. Choose a few different canopy materials to test, such as foil, a plastic bag, tissue paper, and copy paper. Use the picture above to help you create your parachute models. Drop them one by one from your testing point. You may want to have a friend or an adult help you time how long it takes for each to fall.

Plan and Create Your Parachute

Using the information you gathered during testing, draw a plan for the parachute you think will work best. How big should it be? Will you use one material, or a combination of materials? Build the parachute based on your plan.

Once you've finished constructing your parachute, try dropping it at least three times. Does it take the same amount of time to fall during each drop? What is the parachute's average speed?

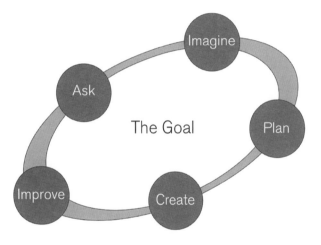

The Goal

Imagine

Ask

Plan

Improve

Create

Improve Your Parachute

Can you make your parachute fall more slowly? What is the slowest rate of speed you can achieve? Once you are satisfied with the speed of your parachute, can you improve its accuracy? Choose a spot below your dropping point and mark it with an X of tape. Try dropping your parachute three times to see how close it gets to the spot. What changes might you make to your parachute so that it hits the X each time it is dropped?

See What Others Have Done

See what other kids have done at http://www.mos.org/eie/tryit. What did you try? You can submit your solutions and pictures to our website, and maybe we'll post your submission!

Glossary

Aerospace Engineering: The branch of engineering that designs objects that go into space, as well as other crafts that fly, such as airplanes.

Atmosphere: The layer of gases surrounding some planets and moons.

Betelgeuse: A red-colored star in the Orion constellation. Pronounced *BEE-tel-jooz*.

Canopy: The part of a parachute that is pushed open by air or atmosphere and creates drag.

***Capuaçu*:** A coconut-sized fruit. Capuaçu is used to make sweet juices, ice creams, and other desserts. Pronounced *cap-OO-ah-coo*.

Drag: The force of the gases in the atmosphere pushing against an object that is moving.

Engineer: A person who uses his or her creativity and understanding of mathematics and science to design things that solve problems.

Engineering Design Process: The steps that engineers use to design something to solve a problem.

***Feijoada*:** A pork-and-bean-based stew known as the national dish of Brazil. Pronounced *faysh-WAH-dah*.

Load: The mass being carried.

Mãe: Portuguese word for mother. Pronounced *MAY*.

Oi: Casual Portuguese word for hello. Pronounced *OI* as in joy.

Orion: A constellation named after the hunter Orion from Greek mythology. Pronounced *oh-RYE-on*.

Pai: Portuguese word for father. Pronounced *PIE*.

Parachute: A technology used to slow the falling of an object through the air or atmosphere.

Paraquedas: Portuguese word for parachute. Pronounced *par-a-KAY-das*.

Rigel: A bright star in the Orion constellation. Pronounced *RYE-jel*.

Southern Cross: A cross-shaped constellation that can be seen from the southern half of Earth.

Suspension Lines: The cords or strings attaching a load to a parachute.

Technology: Any thing or process that people create and use to solve a problem.